IMAGES
of America

PETALUMA
CALIFORNIA

Simone Wilson

ARCADIA
PUBLISHING

Copyright © 2001 by Simone Wilson
ISBN 978-1-5316-1288-7

Published by Arcadia Publishing
Charleston, South Carolina

Library of Congress Catalog Card Number: 2001091344

For all general information contact Arcadia Publishing at:
Telephone 843-853-2070
Fax 843-853-0044
E-mail sales@arcadiapublishing.com
For customer service and orders:
Toll-Free 1-888-313-2665

Visit us on the Internet at www.arcadiapublishing.com

Contents

Acknowledgments		6
Introduction		7
1.	Native Americans and Ranchos	9
2.	The Town at Creek's End	15
3.	Golden Fields and Cooling Fog	25
4.	The Age of Industry	45
5.	Getting Goods to Market	49
6.	Evolution of a City	61
7.	Keeping Shop	77
8.	Military Tradition	93
9.	Civic Institutions and the Big Scoop	97
10.	The Social Round	113

Acknowledgments

Thanks to Keith Ulrich, my editor at Arcadia Publishing, for guidance and forbearance when deadlines loomed. I am grateful to Sherman Boivin and Lee Torliatt for their recollections of Petaluma in earlier days. Thanks also to curator Courtney Clements of the Sonoma County Museum for permission to scour the archives for photographs. I am also indebted to two Petaluma historians, the late Ed Mannion and the late Ed Fratini, some of whose photos now enhance the collection of the Petaluma Historical Museum. Above all, this project could not have proceeded so smoothly without the cheerful assistance and encouragement of both volunteers and staff at the Petaluma Historical Museum, especially Althea Torliatt, Hoppy Hopkins, Lucy Kortum, and museum director Debi Riddle.

—Simone Wilson

INTRODUCTION

The river comes in and the river goes back out—this was the central fact that dictated the ebb and flow of life in early Petaluma. For the Petaluma River is not really a flowing river but a tidal arm of San Francisco Bay, and Petalumans, who depended on the waterway for commerce, had to attune themselves to its rhythm.

The Miwoks, who have inhabited the region for several thousand years, depended on seasonal rhythms for their livelihood—taking fish and shellfish from the water, plants and acorns from the land. Hunters searching for food at the time of the Gold Rush followed the creek to its northern end and set up camp there. Their cabins gave way to warehouses, and slowly a diverse and prosperous town developed on the riverbank. Boats with shallow drafts, designed for sloughs and mudflats, brought people and freight, and they carried away the products that turned Petaluma into a prosperous hub.

In some ways, Petaluma followed the same evolution as other California cities. Spanish and then Mexican ranchos were taken over by waves of American settlers, who then formed incorporated towns starting in the 1850s. But Petaluma's unique topography also made it distinct from other fledgling towns. The river provided a natural link with the city of San Francisco, a ready-made market for the fresh local products—eggs, dairy, and produce—that flowed in from the rich surrounding farmland. Neighboring towns like Penngrove, Cotati, and Two Rock funneled their products through Petaluma, helping shape its role as a thriving commercial center.

That commerce made Petaluma relatively rich for a small town, and the resulting prosperity made possible the other elements that characterize the town: the banks, parks, bustling hotels, lively businesses, and stately Victorian homes.

New modes of transport—the railroad and then the motor car—came to Petaluma, and again the town altered to accommodate them, while continuing to employ the river on its doorstep. Petaluma was the last waterway in the state to have regular sternwheeler traffic, the final voyage being in 1950.

Just as the river came and went, so industries shifted over the decades. Chicken ranches once boomed in the region, supplying eggs for the biggest hatcheries in the world. Dairy farms produced the milk for large enterprises like Alpha Creamery. Together those twin industries gave rise to the Butter and Egg Days that Petaluma still celebrates each spring. Today chicken ranches and dairy farms still prosper, but the egg business as an industry has shifted elsewhere. High-tech industries have congregated in the newest part of town, east of the freeway, and who knows what will replace them as technology shifts and shifts again in this new millennium?

A community, like any extended family, continues to adapt and evolve. A book of photographs gives us a glimpse of the town as it was, with its businesses and characters, its streets and schools. Even as we move ahead, a tour of the past can provide the perspective to envision the future as we would like it to be.

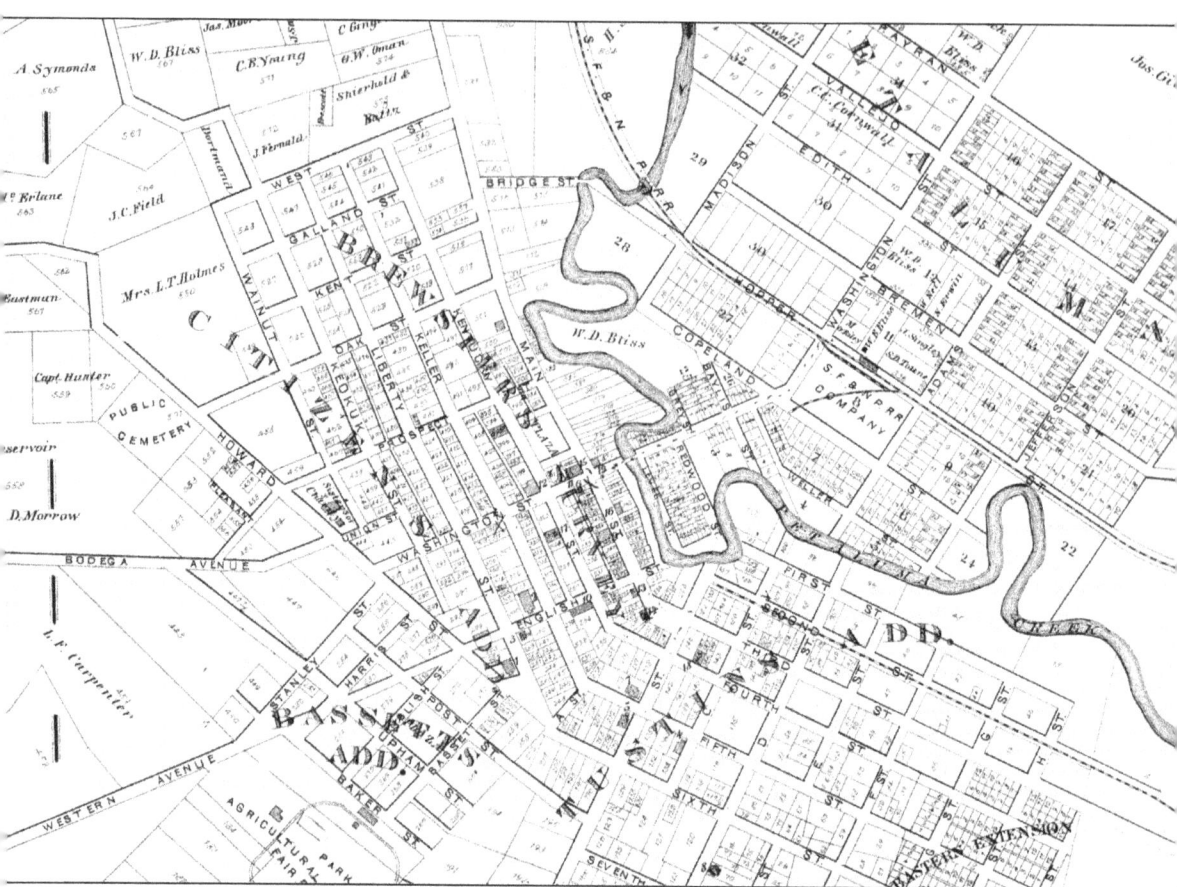

The City of Petaluma, from the Thompson Atlas of 1877, with the river snaking through the middle of town. North is at the top. Note that the river is identified as Petaluma Creek. The "creek" was upgraded to a "river" in 1959 so the waterway would qualify for government funding for dredging.

One

NATIVE AMERICANS AND RANCHOS

Between 5,000 and 8,000 years ago, the Coast Miwok people moved into what are now Marin and southern Sonoma Counties. They enjoyed a prosperous life in a land with a mild climate and abundant natural resources: fish and shellfish in the rivers and bays, deer and elk in the hills, and acorns from the oak woodlands. They made tule boats to explore inland waterways and traded with the Pomo and other neighboring tribes. Pictured above is the 1822 lithograph, *Dance Headgear of the Inhabitants of California*, by Louis Choris. (Courtesy University of Alaska, Fairbanks, Rasmuson Library.)

The Russian colony at Fort Ross and Bodega Bay, which lasted from 1812 to 1841, employed both Miwok and Pomo people. The Russians, who were curious about native peoples, collected baskets and sketched the people they encountered, including this ink and watercolor portrait of Valtazar, a young man of the North Bay, by Mikhail Tikhanov, 1818. (Courtesy University of Alaska, Fairbanks, Rasmuson Library.)

The arrival of Spanish, Mexican, and American settlers disrupted the life of the Miwok. The newcomers imposed their own concept of property rights on the land, putting up fences and grazing livestock. By the 1840s, the North Bay's native peoples had dwindled drastically, many killed by epidemics of smallpox, for which they had no immunity. Those remaining, largely stripped of their land and way of life, found work on ranches. During the Mexican era, only one rancho in California was owned by a Native American; Camilo Ynitia, a Coast Miwok, owned Olompali Rancho between Petaluma and Novato. Above is a recreation of a typical Miwok-style reed boat crossing San Francisco Bay c. 1980. (Courtesy East Bay Regional Park Service.)

Despite these hardships, the Coast Miwok have preserved their identity and in 2001 regained their tribal status when the U.S. Congress recognized them as the Federated Coast Miwok. Today their way of life is recreated and celebrated in such places as Olompali Park, the Kule Loklo village at Point Reyes (above), and the Marin Museum of the American Indian in Novato. MAPOM (Miwok Archaeological Preserve of Marin), located in San Rafael, publishes books on Miwok history and culture and also gives classes in traditional Miwok arts, including tool-making and food preparation (right). (Courtesy Petaluma Museum.)

The rich alluvial land along Petaluma Creek (above, looking south) was a natural spot for a prosperous rancho. The Mexican government in 1833 appointed Mariano G. Vallejo as commandant of the Northern Frontier. Authorized to parcel out the land north of San Francisco Bay, Vallejo allotted 44,000 choice acres to himself, creating the Petaluma Rancho. Other grants, covering much of today's Sonoma County, went to Vallejo's brothers-in-law and others who had assisted the Mexican government. In 1844 Juan Miranda claimed the land west of Petaluma Creek, including the land that is now downtown Petaluma.

Although he maintained an official headquarters in the garrison town of Sonoma, Vallejo (left) had a two-story adobe home built on the eastern side of Petaluma Valley starting in 1836. Most of the work was done by Indian laborers from the Sonoma and San Rafael missions. The adobe and the estate surrounding it were like a small village, with its own food supply, herds of sheep and cattle, blacksmith, tannery, craftsmen, and farm laborers. Vallejo also employed Yankee settlers, who had begun to trickle in from the East. Beleaguered by increasing numbers of squatters, Vallejo sold the adobe in 1857. (Courtesy Sonoma Valley Historical Society.)

The state acquired the adobe in 1951, and today the restored home is the centerpiece of a State Historic Park. Every summer the Parks Department recreates the flavor of rancho life during Adobe Days, with demonstrations of blacksmithing and other activities of the mid-19th century (right). The discovery of gold in the California foothills, combined with the transference of California from Mexico to the U.S., spelled the end of the rancho era and the emergence of towns founded by Yankee settlers. Hunters gathering food for the miners in San Francisco set up camp at the headwaters of the Petaluma Creek in 1850 to shoot deer, geese, and even grizzlies and then built wharves and warehouses to house their goods. (Courtesy Petaluma Museum.)

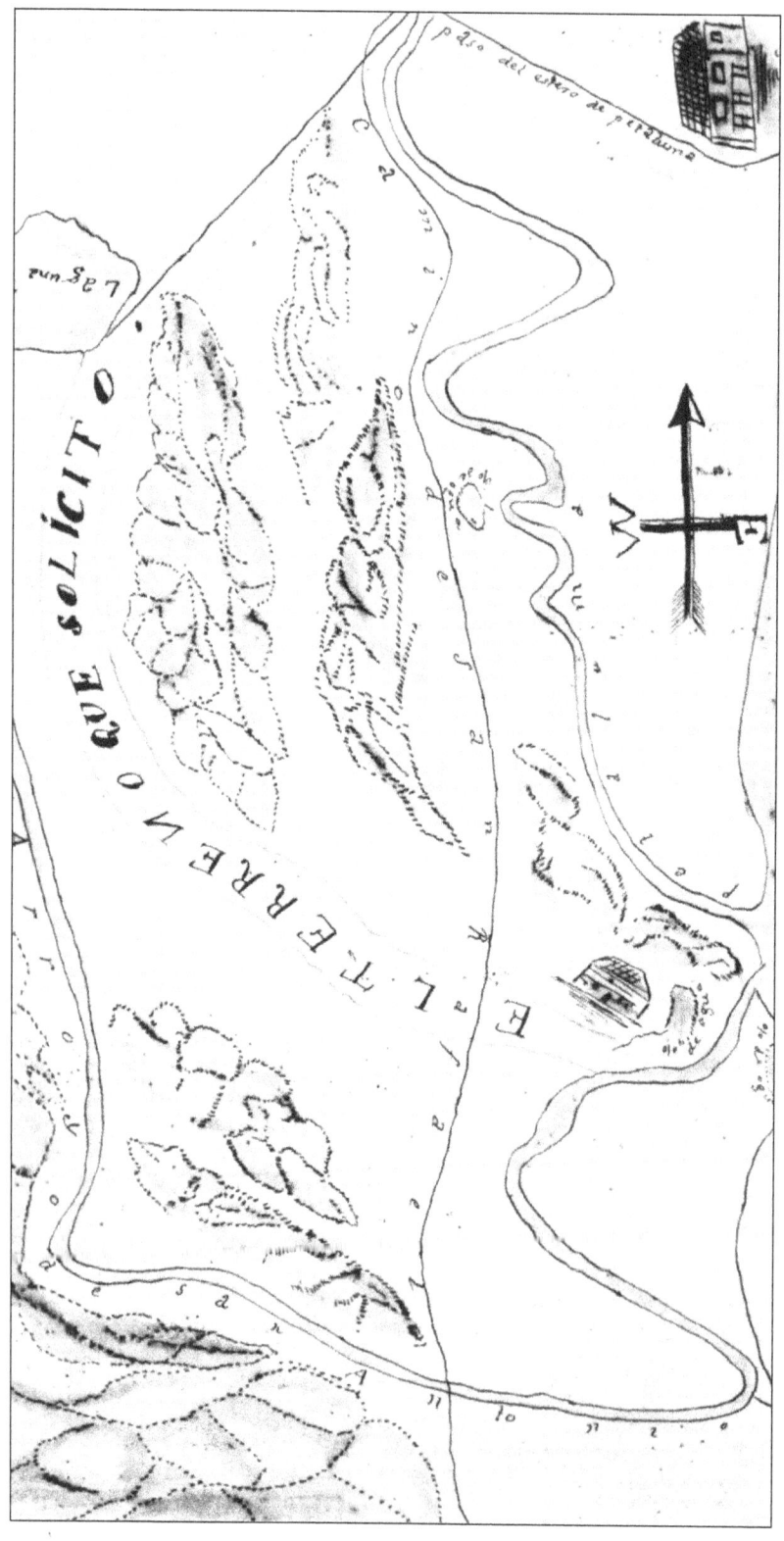

In 1844 Juan Miranda filed this sketch in his application for Rancho Arroyo de San Antonio. His house is at lower right, with Vallejo's adobe in the upper right. Miranda's boundaries were San Antonio Creek to the west and south, and Petaluma Creek on the east. In 1848 California became U.S. territory; squatters set up homes on Miranda's rancho. Garrett Keller claimed 158 acres of choice land beside the creek and then sold lots in fledgling Petaluma at $10 apiece. The town incorporated in 1858. The U.S. Supreme Court did not confirm Miranda's claim until 1873.

Two

THE TOWN AT CREEK'S END

The first steamer *Gold* plied the route from Petaluma down to San Pablo Bay. Built in 1883, she burned to the waterline on November 8, 1920 at Steamer Gold Landing (the *Gold* was named not for the metal but for one of its owners, Captain Gold). Flat-bottomed scows and steamers like the *Gold* and the *Petaluma* carried the freight that made Petaluma into a prosperous river town. By 1900 the creek was the third busiest waterway in California. Actually a tidal estuary, Petaluma Creek was renamed Petaluma River in 1959 in order to qualify for funding for dredging. (Courtesy Petaluma Museum.)

Until the railroad came in 1870, the creek was the only avenue of commerce to markets in San Francisco. Savvy river pilots took ships like the *Margarete* (above) across the bay and then braved 14 twisting miles of shallow estuary to reach the Petaluma docks. Here ships are tied up at the wharves to load hay, potatoes from Bodega, and eggs. The McNear brothers built their first brick warehouse in 1864. McNear's mill (above right), now called the Great Mill, is full of shops and cafes today. (Courtesy Petaluma Museum.)

Charles Minturn, 1815–1873, known as the Ferryboat King of San Francisco, operated a fleet of steamboats on the Sacramento River and assorted inlets of San Francisco Bay. In 1862 he paid to have two bends in Petaluma Creek straightened out and put the *E. Corning* and the *Kate Hayes* into service along the creek. He then established a monopoly on steamer service along Petaluma Creek and jacked up the fares and the mail rates, making himself universally disliked in town. (Courtesy Bancroft Library.)

The steamer *Gold* was operated by the Petaluma and Santa Rosa Railway. This railroad also owned the last sternwheeler in the western U.S., the *Petaluma*, which made its final run in 1950. Boats faced a variety of hazards. Captain Thompson of the *Georgiana* overtaxed the boiler and his steamboat blew up at the dock at the foot of Western Avenue in November 1855. Some craft succumbed to fire, like the second *Petaluma*, which burned at the dock in 1914. Schooners and steamers sometimes sank in mid-stream, threatening other shipping. (Ed Mannion collection, courtesy Petaluma Museum.)

Christian Jacobsen (center) and two other boatmen work on a boat on the banks of Petaluma Creek, c. 1900. Jacobsen was first mate on the *Robert W. Hind*, owned by Capt. Robert Dollar, a Bay Area railroad magnate. (Courtesy Petaluma Museum.)

Farmers and townspeople took to the river in small craft to fish and hunt waterfowl. Notice the ship in the main channel in the background. (Courtesy Petaluma Museum.)

Lumber is stacked up at Golden Eagle Milling Co., site of the Turning Basin. Besides lumber, a good deal of hay and produce made its way to the Petaluma docks for shipment to the city. Eventually Petaluma also was the railhead for freight and passengers headed north, so that Petaluma's hotels were full of travelers. (Courtesy Petaluma Museum.)

In town, boats could pull up along wooden docks, but along the creek south of town, flat-bottomed boats would simply pull up alongside the bank so farmers could bring their hay and other crops aboard. (Courtesy Petaluma Museum.)

Long after the construction of the railroad, many businesses shipped their goods to San Francisco by boat. Warehouses along First Street backed up to the creek, where boats tied up to take on goods. Scow schooners operated until the 1920s, when trucks began to take over most of the freight business.

Schooners with crates piled high on their decks carried goods along the winding tidal creek, carefully navigating the estuary's relatively shallow waters. Thirty schooners regularly made the trip up and down the estuary in the 1880s. (Courtesy Petaluma Museum.)

Both the Gold (above) and the Petaluma went through various incarnations. The first Petaluma, built in 1857, was destroyed in 1900; the second Petaluma burned to the waterline at the Petaluma wharf in 1914 with a full cargo of eggs. The crew pushed it into the stream to save the dock. Its engines went into Petlauma number three, which had its smokestack in the stern so the heat wouldn't poach the eggs on board. (Courtesy Petaluma Museum.)

Capt. Al Bravo was the last captain of the Gold; in this photograph he is aboard the J.D. Peters. The first Gold burned in 1920 and took the dock and warehouse along with it; it was succeeded by Gold No. 2. (Courtesy San Francisco Maritime Museum.)

Townspeople enjoy a stroll across the D Street Bridge, c. 1905. The bridge was built across the creek in 1883 to provide access from downtown to the railroad depot east of the creek. The bridge swung to the side, allowing boats to pass. (Courtesy Harrington family collection.)

The *Newtown* No. 2 waits for her cargo at Hunt and Behrens dock on the west side of the creek upstream from Washington Street. (Courtesy Petaluma Museum.)

Over 2,500 people crowd the docks to watch the steamer *Petaluma* pass under the new D Street drawbridge on its opening day, June 10, 1933. Mayor William J. Farrell was the first to walk across the new steel structure, known as a bascule bridge. (Courtesy Petaluma Museum.)

A boat approaches Golden Eagle Milling at the Turning Basin. H.T. Fairbanks bought Percival Milling in 1888 and changed the name to Golden Eagle, running it with his four sons. They were pioneers in adding vitamins to poultry feed. The mill closed in 1964. (Courtesy Petaluma Museum.)

This aerial photo shows the town in 1937, with the river in the foreground, and McNear Peninsula in the center. (Courtesy Petaluma Museum.)

Captain Jack Urton (left) was the last skipper of the *Petaluma*, which made its last run on August 24, 1950. It was the last commercial sternwheeler in the state. Urton's final entry in the ship's log reads, "Arr. Petaluma 10:45 p.m. . . . . After 35 years, 8 mo., and 10 days, we tie up for good. This ends 103 years of sternwheel river navigation on SF bay and tributaries." (Courtesy Petaluma Museum.)

Three
GOLDEN FIELDS AND COOLING FOG

The alluvial soil of the Petaluma Valley makes it prime agricultural land. Dairy, eggs, and hay formed the basis of Petaluma's agricultural wealth. Carl Plow and his wife, owners of the Alpha Creamery on Washington Street, pose with some of their workers. (Courtesy Petaluma Museum.)

The yard of the Martin ranch, west of town in Chileno Valley, was a busy place in the days before milking barns. Cows were milked in the yard, and the milk was then poured into shallow pans and kept overnight in a cool shed so the cream could be skimmed off in the morning. (Ed Fratini collection, courtesy Petaluma Museum.)

As California's population grew, dairy and produce became ever more valuable. By 1855, butter from Petaluma brought $1.25 a pound in Sacramento. At left are Jersey cows.

Dairymen brought their wagons to the Cooperative Creamery at Western Avenue and Baker Street to unload their milk pails, 1914. Started in 1913, the Cooperative eventually had members from Sonoma, Marin, Napa, Lake, and Mendocino Counties. By 1930, the co-op began shipping milk to San Francisco, generally 50 10-gallons cans per day. (Courtesy Petaluma Museum.)

A worker keeps the equipment going in the churn room at Petaluma Cooperative Creamery, 1939. By 1955, the co-op had 1,300 members with a total of 35,000 cows, and Sonoma County had the second greatest milk production in the state. (Courtesy Petaluma Museum.)

A group of spectators came out to the fields and hitched a ride on this mule-drawn combine harvester, c. 1900. Starting around 1890, the Pacific Reclamation Co. began growing hay on reclaimed marshland in southern Sonoma County. Scows and barges navigated the sloughs south of Petaluma and farther east around Skaggs Island, shipping the hay to the city. (Walter Olsen collection, courtesy Petaluma Museum.)

With all the horse-drawn traffic in San Francisco, the company sold on average 5,000 tons of hay per month. Then in the mid-1920s, most traffic in the city became motorized, and the bottom dropped out of the hay market. (Harrington family collection, courtesy Sonoma County Historical Society.)

The countryside around Petaluma, with its mild climate and occasional coastal fog, was the ideal spot for chicken ranches. People in town often raised small flocks of chickens as well. (Courtesy Petaluma Museum.)

Canadian Lyman Byce came to Petaluma in 1878 to raise Leghorns and Plymouth Rock chickens. He also perfected an incubator, originally invented by local I.L. Dias, calibrating it to maintain a steady temperature. The incubator was a great success at the 1883 California State Fair. By 1897 Byce's Petaluma Incubator Co. (above) had manufactured and sold over 15,000 incubators. (Harrington collection, courtesy Sonoma County Historical Society.)

Byce (left) and Christopher Nisson, an immigrant from Denmark, paved the way for Petaluma's prosperous egg industry. Nisson arrived in 1864 and started a ranch west of town in Two Rock. By the 1880s he owned the region's largest commercial egg ranch. Nisson started using Byce's incubators in 1881. He also developed an improved brooder and founded Petaluma's Pioneer Hatchery, the first commercial hatchery in the nation. Other Petaluma hatcheries, including Poehlman's, Bihn's, and Must Hatchery, followed and Petaluma became a leading center of the poultry business. (Courtesy Petaluma Museum.)

One of the workers at the Petaluma Incubator Co. enjoys a snooze at the factory, 1917. (Harrington collection, courtesy Sonoma County Historical Society.)

Incubators manufactured by the Petaluma Incubator Co. were good for more than just chicken eggs. A number of the cabinets were shipped to South Africa, where ranchers used them to incubate ostrich eggs. The round insert in the lower right shows a herd of ostriches.

By 1917 Petaluma was celebrating its status as a poultry center with an Egg Day Parade. Designed to promote Petaluma's prominence as a prosperous egg center, the parade featured chicken-oriented floats, like the one above, featuring an enormous egg occupied by a local beauty. (Courtesy Petaluma Museum.)

Josephine Durbin, as part of the Bell Telephone contingent, marched in the 1917 Egg Day parade dressed as a Bell telephone receiver. Several other Bell employees followed behind her, dressed as telephone poles. The Petaluma Savings Bank boasted the town's first telephone in 1881, and in 1884 Atwater's store on Main installed a telephone exchange with a magneto switchboard. (Courtesy Petaluma Museum.)

This float, sponsored by the Petaluma Incubator Co., shows an ostrich just emerging from its over-sized shell, pulled by a team of four roosters. Some of the men sport rooster leggings. The Incubator Co. did a thriving business, maintaining offices in San Francisco and Indianapolis. (Courtesy Sonoma County Museum.)

Petaluma's self-promotion went into high gear in 1918, when the town's Chamber of Commerce hired advertising specialist Bert Kerrigan (right, with daughter Herleon). Kerrigan billed Petaluma as the Egg Capital of the World, spending $50,000 on a public relations campaign to publicize the poultry business. National newsreel companies filmed the farms and hatcheries, and Petaluma became famous nationwide as the world's egg basket. (Kerrigan family collection, courtesy Petaluma Museum.)

Farmerettes of 1926 were Jane King, Frances Tassi, Mabel Lounibos, and Anita Reed. Note the eucalyptus trees in the background; eucalyptus were imported from Australia in the 1850s and by the turn of the century had an established role in California as windbreaks and ornamentals. (Courtesy Petaluma Museum.)

Young dancers, their costumes inspired by the diaphanous style of Isadora Duncan, perform for the Egg Day crowd in 1923. (Courtesy Petaluma Museum.)

Emily Spaich, Miss Petaluma of 1923, poses beside a poster for the August Egg Day Fair. In the wake of Kerrigan's publicity campaigns, more ranchers streamed into the Petaluma area to start chicken ranches. (Courtesy Petaluma Museum.)

Improved incubators and brooders made the chicken business more profitable for entrepreneurs like Joseph Buchwald, whose egg packing business was on Bodega Avenue next to the Bihn Hatchery. (Courtesy Petaluma Museum.)

In the heyday of the egg industry, Petalumans loved to keep a tally of eggs sold and chicks hatched. In 1910 the town shipped 7 million dozen eggs to San Francisco. In 1940 the number had risen to 30 million dozen. (Courtesy Petaluma Museum.)

A.E. Bourke brought his family north from Los Angeles in 1898 and established the Must Hatch Incubator Co. Bourke himself went to South America at the request of the U.S. government to help ranchers there improve their poultry production. He sold the hatchery to his son Leo, who turned it into a prosperous incubator factory. The original building burned down in 1923; the 1927 Spanish Renaissance Revival structure that replaced it (above) was built in 1927 at the corner of 7th and F Streets. (Courtesy Petaluma Museum.)

The Crown Prince of Sweden, seeing the sights of California in 1922, came away from his tour of the Must Hatch Incubator Co. with a flat of chicks. (Courtesy Petaluma Museum.)

William L. Sales established Sales Hatchery on 3rd Street in 1888. The business was destroyed by fire in 1932 and Sales merged in 1935 with Bourke's Must Hatch Hatchery. By the 1950s, Sales and Bourke's was selling chickens in 11 western states. (Courtesy Petaluma Museum.)

Frank Poehlman, once a partner of Bourke, started his own hatchery before World War I. After the war, his son Max joined him in the business. Frank Poehlman died in 1922, and his widow and Max ran the business until 1930, when she sold her interest to her son-in-law, Nat Thompson. Poehlman's was one of the more successful hatcheries, also operating a branch in Salt Lake City. (Courtesy Petaluma Museum.)

Women performed a labor-intensive job—washing eggs in one of Petaluma's many hatcheries. (Courtesy Sonoma County Museum.)

Colony-style chicken houses were a familiar sight in the region all around Petaluma and are still seen today, especially west of town. (Courtesy Sonoma County Museum.)

Packers fit eggs into cardboard dividers for shipping, adapting assembly-line techniques to the egg business. The man in the left rear, wearing a suit, is John J. Bergstadt, president of the Poultry Producers of Central California. The PPCC moved to San Leandro in the 1950s. (Courtesy Petaluma Museum.)

If a town has enough chickens, the birds rate their own drug store. Started in 1923 by James Keyes (in doorway), the Chicken Pharmacy on Main was featured in a February 1939 *National Geographic* article and also appeared in *Ripley's Believe It or Not* as the world's only drug store devoted solely to poultry. (Courtesy Petaluma Museum.)

The Chicken Pharmacy sold chicken vaccines, delouser, and the pharmacy's own special "pullet pills." In 1926 Dr. Davis (left), a poultry expert, became Keyes' partner in the business and took over as sole owner in 1933. At its height the pharmacy dispensed 50,000 doses of pullet pills and other medications a day. (Courtesy Petaluma Museum.)

Frances Tassi gives Charlotte Ellsworth Petaluma's signature hair treatment—an egg shampoo, possibly as a promotion for one of the Egg Day parades, 1926. (Courtesy Petaluma Museum.)

A king-sized display near the train depot proclaims Petaluma the World's Egg Basket, having produced 35 million dozen eggs in 1925. (Courtesy Sonoma County Museum.)

Four

THE AGE OF INDUSTRY

Eggs were not Petaluma's only industrialized commodity. In 1868, a soap factory was established. In 1892 the Carlson and Currier Co. bought land from John McNear and built a Georgian Colonial-style silk mill. Using silk imported from China, the mill could process 250 pounds of raw silk per day. (Courtesy Petaluma Museum.)

Women made up the bulk of the silk mill's work force. Spoolers sat in regimented rows, winding silk for market. The factory produced knitting silk, embroidery silk, and hosiery. Belding Brothers, a later owner, doubled the size of the building. In 1940 the Sunset Line and Twine Co. purchased the factory at Jefferson and Erwin to manufacture fishing line and other types of twine. (Courtesy Petaluma Museum.)

With the egg industry being such a large factor in the prosperity of Petaluma, auxiliary businesses also thrived, including Adam's Box Factory at Edith and Jefferson, where a worker assembles cardboard dividers to keep eggs from breaking during shipping. (Courtesy Petaluma Museum.)

With industry came the beginnings of the modern office, like the one here at M. Vonsen Co., c. 1918. From left to right are Caroline Jensen Doss, Marie Pronini Glahn, Ruby Rasmussen Murphy, Herman Hazlett, Magnus Vonsen (the boss), and Miles Murphy. (Courtesy Petaluma Museum.)

Petaluma missed the winery boom that swept over much of Sonoma County, but the Petaluma U.S. Brewery did a thriving business before 1920, when Prohibition put a damper on Sonoma County's thriving alcohol businesses. The Petaluma Brewery started on Main Street in 1855, not long after the creation of the town itself. Inside the brewery, Eivers Anderson (left, in apron) boxes some of the capped bottles. (Courtesy Petaluma Museum.)

Five

GETTING GOODS TO MARKET

Transport was vital for marketing all the eggs being laid, chicks hatched, and grain harvested. Petaluma was also the hub where cities to the north sent goods to be shipped across the Bay. The natural avenue of transport was the river, but wagons, railroads, and finally trucks played their part. Farnsworth & Sons Drayage, above, loaded goods onto a "low-boy" in front of Dodge, Sweeney and Co. Manager Peter J. Blin is standing in front. (Ed Fratini collection, courtesy Petaluma Museum.)

Transporting goods from factory to customer required skilled loading. In front of the Petaluma Incubator Co., a driver checks a shipment of incubators ultimately bound for Australia. (Ed Fratini collection, courtesy Petaluma Museum.)

A town with so many hatcheries required a constant supply of chicken feed for ranchers. Workers at George P. McNear's mill kept ranchers supplied with the feed they needed. (Ed Fratini collection, courtesy Petaluma Museum.)

The broad gauge train pulls into the NWP depot on its way north. Petaluma's first railroad, built by ferry mogul Charles Minturn in 1862, started at Haystack, near today's Marina. Two years later its locomotive blew up when the engineer forgot to check the boiler; after that mules pulled the train the two miles to town. In the 1870s Peter Donohue built the broad gauge through East Petaluma, the portion of town east of the river. Today this part of town is called Old East Petaluma, since people generally call the area east of Highway 101 East Petaluma. (Loraine Owens collection, courtesy Petaluma Museum.)

The Northwestern Pacific railroad depot, which still sits on Lakeville Highway, is a classic of the Mission Revival style. It was built in 1914, on the site where railroad magnate Peter Donohue had constructed an earlier depot. Passenger service ceased in the 1940s, but NWP continued to use the building as a freight office. The white roof in the middle distance belongs to the Steamer Gold landing. (Courtesy Petaluma Museum.)

The broad gauge passes the Petaluma Hotel (later called the Tivoli) in 1941. (Courtesy Petaluma Museum.)

Businessmen drive the first spike for the Petaluma and Santa Rosa Electric Railway on April 5, 1904. The electric railway connected Petaluma with Sebastopol. From there branches went east to Santa Rosa and north to Forestville. Nicknamed the Chicken and Cow Line, the railway was built to help outlying towns get their produce to market via Petaluma's rail and shipping lines. The man in the center with a cigar in his right hand is Art Newburg, reporter for the *Argus*. (Ed Fratini collection, courtesy Petaluma Museum.)

Passengers rush to catch the P&SR from Santa Rosa to Petaluma. By the 1920s the P&SR was running 12 round trips a day between Petaluma and Sebastopol, 19 a day between Sebastopol and Santa Rosa, and 16 from Sebastopol north to Forestville and back. (Courtesy Sonoma County Museum.)

A wagon driver waits for the arrival of the P&SR at its station at Washington and Copeland. Passengers bound for San Francisco got off the train and walked a block to catch the boat at the Steamer Gold landing. (Courtesy Petaluma Museum.)

Bill Parks was the conductor and Chris Christensen the driver on a run of the Petaluma and Santa Rosa railway. The P&SR carried a wide range of passengers—rural kids bound for junior high and high school in Petaluma, older students bound for college in Santa Rosa, farmers going to market. In 1932, the NWP took over the P&SR and passenger service was discontinued. (Ed Fratini collection, courtesy Petaluma Museum.)

The first P&SR passenger cars were painted white, but they proved too hard to keep clean, so the company switched to yellow with a red stripe. Here passengers wait outside the train in Forestville.

Car cleaner Peter Sciaroni takes a break inside a P&SR car en route from Petaluma to Santa Rosa, c. 1915. The P&SR was not known for paying high wages, and employees sometimes referred to the company as the "Poor and Stingy." (Courtesy Petaluma Museum.)

P&SR's diesel locomotive No. 3 travels past Petaluma's Yosemite Hotel, c. 1960. Although the advent of automobiles spelled the end of passenger service on the P&SR, freight service continued into the 1980s, serving rural stations between Petaluma and Sebastopol such as Orchard Station, Turner Station, and Cunningham. (Ed Mannion collection, courtesy Petaluma Museum.)

Horse-drawn streetcar service began around 1890 and lasted about a decade. The route started on F Street, proceeded along Sixth and then turned down Western. It then went along Kentucky and turned east on Washington. The streetcar generally turned at the train depot for the return trip, but for special events it continued on to Kenilworth Park. Owner N.R. Peters charged 5¢ for a ride, but he had a soft spot for children and often let them hop on for free, especially if they were running errands for their parents. (Courtesy Petaluma Museum.)

Fred Wiseman (seated near dog) made history on February 17, 1911, taking off in his plane from Petaluma's Kenilworth Park with 3 stamped letters and 50 copies of the Santa Rosa *Press Democrat*. His flight to the Sonoma County Fairgrounds 14 miles away was the world's first confirmed airmail flight. Wiseman was a Santa Rosa racecar driver who built a plane after meeting the Wright Brothers. By 1930 he had abandoned flying, convinced it had a limited future, and returned to automotive engineering. His plane is now in the Smithsonian. (Courtesy Sonoma County Museum.)

The Petaluma airport, now on Skyranch Drive, was a small operation in 1935. Also home of the Two-Niner Diner, it is located east of town. (Courtesy Petaluma Museum.)

George P. McNear and family go out for a ride in the family car. As private automobiles became popular, they replaced passenger service on trains like the local Petaluma and Santa Rosa electric railway. (Courtesy Petaluma Museum.)

An early freight truck parks in front of the Farrell building. Notice the canvas side, rolled up and tied near the roofline, in place of a driver's side door. William F. Farrell was a blacksmith who turned to auto and truck repairs as engines replaced horse-drawn transport. His sons, A.H. and William J. Farrell, assisted him in the business. (Courtesy Petaluma Museum.)

Autos replaced wagons as the means of transporting goods around town. Here cars and trucks line up to collect feed sacks at NcNear's feed mill, at the corner of Main and B Streets, c. 1930. (Courtesy Petaluma Museum.)

In 1912 this vehicle brought a load of three tons of Parrot Brand Soap from Philadelphia to the Carlson Currier mill, making the first transcontinental motorized truck delivery. The trip was sponsored by the truck maker, the American Locomotive Co. (Courtesy Petaluma Museum.)

Before the freeway was built in the 1950s, Old Redwood Highway, shown here at the south end of town, was the main route into Petaluma from San Francisco. In town the highway became Third Street. Between B Street and Washington it was called Main St., and north of Washington it was called North Main. Note the Flying A sign at lower right. (Courtesy Petaluma Museum.)

The Highway 101 Bridge spanning the Petaluma River south of town was still under construction in this 1955 photo. (Courtesy Petaluma Museum.)

Six

EVOLUTION OF A CITY

Main Street (now Petaluma Boulevard) runs through the heart of Petaluma's downtown. The center of town evolved from a dusty thoroughfare with hitching rails to the heart of a modern city. The picture above shows Main near Western, looking north. In center rear is the tower of the Masonic Building, begun in 1871. When journalist Bayard Taylor arrived by boat in 1859 he noted that Petaluma had roughly 2,500 inhabitants, and that, "the air of business and prosperity which it wears is quite striking."

By the 1880s, Petaluma's population had risen to 5,000. Above is Main Street in the heart of downtown c. 1890, with wagons and hitching rails. The light-colored building in the center is the 1886 McNear building. The Cosmopolitan Hotel to its right is now a parking lot, while the small wooden building to its left was Murphy's Meat Market. That was replaced in 1911 by a southern extension to the McNear Building. (Courtesy Petaluma Museum.)

Stores along the south side of B Street between Main and 4th Street, 1902, included (left to right) Case's Horse Shoeing, a Tamale Parlor serving chili con carne, Henry Myer's Eagle Saloon, and a grocery store. Today most of the block is occupied by Rex Ace Hardware, originally owned by the Hobbie family and run since the 1950s by the Tomasinis. The stair step roofline on the right is clearly visible today at the corner of B and 4th. (Courtesy Petaluma Museum.)

The 1906 earthquake damaged this building at Main and Washington, and steamer *Gold* returned to the Petaluma dock with most of its cargo of eggs broken. However, no one died in Petaluma, and the *Argus* commented, "Most of the buildings wrecked were ancient affairs which should have been condemned years ago." Petalumans sent wagons with supplies to heavily damaged Santa Rosa, and several Petaluma doctors went to San Francisco to help the injured.

For Christmas c. 1918, townspeople gathered for a public celebration on Main Street; note the Christmas tree in the center. (Courtesy Petaluma Museum.)

Downtown traffic was already lively in this 1920s photo of Western and Main (now Petaluma Boulevard) looking north. On the left is the 1926 American Trust Co. building, designed in Neoclassical Revival style by San Francisco architects Hyman and Appleton. In 1960 the building became Wells Fargo bank and is now an antique store. (Courtesy Petaluma Museum.)

William J. Farrell, Petaluma's mayor from 1929 to 1933, helped the town use its assets to weather the Depression. Farrell was the son of blacksmith William F. Farrell, who arrived in Petaluma in the 1860s and opened a blacksmith shop. His sons William James and A.H. Farrell worked in the business and after World War I became the local agents for Dodge cars. During World War II, Farrell served as a civil defense official; he died in 1942 following an auto accident near Dillon Beach. (Courtesy Petaluma Museum.)

The 1882 Masonic Building (left) at Western and Main, a Victorian Italianate building with cast iron features, is one of the Western Avenue Ironfronts. The row continues with two 1885 buildings—Dom Ivana and Andresen's—and ends at Kentucky Street with the three-story Mutual Relief Building (far right), also built in 1885. Ironfronts were thought to be resistant to quakes and fires until the 1906 quake destroyed most of San Francisco's ironfronts. Petaluma's are a fortunate survival and are among the state's architectural gems. (Photo by Simone Wilson.)

Snow covers the distant hills in this overview of town east of the river, taken from the top of the American Trust Co. Building on Jan. 22, 1932. (Ed Fratini collection, courtesy Petaluma Museum.)

Center Park was developed around 1910, filling a wide spot on Main Street that had been used for hitching horses and wagons. This panoramic photo from the 1950s shows most of the west side of the street between B Street and Western Avenue. The McNear Building dominates the left side of the photo. The original McNear Building is a Victorian Italianate edifice with ironfront features; it was built in 1886 by John A. McNear, one of Petaluma's most successful merchants. McNear arrived in Petaluma in 1856, prospered in the real estate business, and then branched out into milling and shipping. His son George McNear, who ran McNear's Feed Mill, added a south wing in 1911. Both portions of the building extend all the way from Main Street (now Petaluma Boulevard North) to Fourth Street and have entrances on both streets. For many years the building was boarded up, but in the 1970s Jeff Harriman and Wallace Lourdeaux bought and restored it, transforming it into one of the historic showpieces of downtown Petaluma. Offices fill the upstairs; McNear's Saloon occupies the ground floor

of the 1886 section. The theatre on the ground floor of the 1911 side was originally called the Mystic and was one of California's earliest silent movie houses. After a fire destroyed the Mystic, it was rebuilt as the State, whose vertical marquee is visible in the photo. In the 1970s and 80s it was the site of the Plaza, a popular venue for foreign and avant garde films, and in the 1990s it became a music club called, appropriately, the Mystic.

At upper right is the downtown's signature clock tower. The Seth Thomas Clock with cast iron Roman numerals came from Connecticut around the Horn and was lifted into the ornate tower of the 1882 Masonic Building. When it was installed, the *Argus* declared the clock would be "a positive conservator of public morals," since children would get to school on time, men could pawn their watches, and wives could check on what time their husbands came home. By 1934 the original tower had deteriorated badly; a new one with copper sheathing was constructed and is still in use today. The clock itself is the original. (Courtesy Petaluma Museum.)

Cars stream through Petaluma's bustling downtown in the 1950s. Penney's department store is on the right; behind that is one of the downtown's most imposing landmarks, the clock tower atop the Masonic Building. (Courtesy Petaluma Museum.)

The grain elevator that still dominates the Petaluma skyline was built in 1937. Situated on the east side of Petaluma Creek just upstream from Washington Avenue, the 110-foot structure originally served the Poultry Producers Cooperative of Central California before their move to San Leandro.

Dr. Louis Hilmer and his family lived in this rambling home on J Street between Sunnyslope and Grant Avenue. The doctor holds one of the family children; another climbed onto the balcony for this group picture. (Courtesy Petaluma Museum.)

This fairly typical small farmhouse off Bodega Avenue belonged to Walter Thomas and his wife Anne, who is standing on the porch, c. 1920. The couple were poultry ranchers. (Courtesy Petaluma Museum.)

The Byce family lived in one of Petaluma's posh homes, at 226 Liberty Street. Lyman Byce was a key figure in the town's poultry boom. The house also starred in the 1985 film *Peggy Sue Got Married*. (Courtesy Petaluma Museum.)

The more modest home of the Vonsens, owners of Vonsen Feed store, was on D Street.

The Dennis Healy home at the corner of Washington and Keokuk was one of Petaluma's grand homes. The building, designed by famed local architect Brainerd Jones around 1910, was later used as Sorenson's Funeral home. (Mert Doss collection, courtesy Petaluma Museum.)

Architect Brainerd Jones moved to Petaluma in 1875 at age six, studied in San Francisco, and returned in 1900 to open his own office in Petaluma. His Petaluma works include the Carnegie Library (now Petaluma Museum), the Byce house, the 1911 addition to the McNear Building, and four brick homes on D Street. Nine structures he designed or worked on are on the National Register of Historic Places. (Courtesy Petaluma Museum.)

The Whitney home at 312 6th Street displays a number of intriguing architectural features, including upstairs front rooms with conical roofs. Palm trees, usually associated with southern California, are not uncommon ornamentals in Petaluma. (Courtesy Petaluma Museum.)

Nellie, Catherine, and Carrie Denman sit in the parlor of the Whitney home on Sixth Street. The Denmans, descendants of one of Petaluma's pioneer families, were related to Annabelle St. John Whitney, the wife of Arthur Whitney. The interior shows a typical formal parlor, with family portraits above the ornate fireplace. (Courtesy Petaluma Museum.)

The house at 10 Liberty Street, a Stick Style Queen Anne home built in the late 1880s, was once a rooming house. At one time scheduled for demolition, it was restored and is now one of the many architectural treasures of the A Street Historic District, a six-block area of stately homes constructed between 1860 and 1925. The district is bounded by Western Avenue, Liberty Street, Sixth Street, D Street, and Fourth Street. (Courtesy Petaluma Museum.)

Mel's Drive-In was one of several Petaluma locations for *American Graffiti*, George Lucas' 1973 film of teenage antics during one long summer night. The film starred Richard Dreyfuss, Ron Howard, and Harrison Ford. (Courtesy Petaluma Museum.)

The hills near Adobe Road provided the setting for *The Farmer's Daughter*, 1947, with Loretta Young and Joseph Cotten. With its historic downtown, stately homes, and pristine countryside, Petaluma has attracted film companies since the silent era and is also the setting for numerous commercials. (Courtesy Petaluma Museum.)

Actor Mark Harmon leaves the American Trust Co. in the 1991 remake of *Shadow of a Doubt*. In 1942 Alfred Hitchcock filmed the original version in Santa Rosa, but by the 1990s Santa Rosa's downtown had lost its small-town charm, and Petaluma was chosen as the perfect stand-in. (Courtesy Petaluma Museum.)

Besides its architectural gems, Petaluma still retains much of its waterfront heritage. The 1989 Balshaw walking bridge over the river provides pedestrian access to both sides of the water as well as a great view of boats tied up where McNear's warehouse used to be. (Courtesy Petaluma Museum.)

The *Alma*, the last remaining scow of the four hundred that used to bring goods to town, now belongs to the National Maritime Museum and comes up to Petaluma for River Days in August. (Courtesy Petaluma Museum.)

Seven
KEEPING SHOP

William Zartman and John Fritsch opened a wagon and blacksmith shop at 119 Petaluma Boulevard, next to the American Hotel. Like many early Petalumans, Zartman came to California for the gold rush but found a better living after settling in a town. The shop later moved to Howard and Western, where Zartman's son, William H. Zartman, built up the family business into the largest blacksmith, foundry, and wagon-making business in the county. (Courtesy Sonoma County Museum.)

Charles Wilson's harness shop was one of several businesses that provided equipment for horses and wagons.

Peter Dalessi (left) works in his tire shop with an employee named Linar, c. 1900. (Courtesy Petaluma Museum.)

George Van Bebber was the blacksmith and his brother Fred was the woodworker at Van Bebber's Blacksmith and Wagon Repair, which opened in 1901 on East Washington, shown here in 1914. In 1905 Fred began to make the transition to auto repairs, a decision with real foresight, considering Petaluma then had only seven automobiles. (Courtesy Petaluma Museum.)

The forge at the Van Bebber brothers' resembles any blacksmith shop of the early 1900s. By 1918, Van Bebber's was thriving as a car repair business and the brothers moved to Main Street. In 1919, however, Fred became ill, and they sold out to Pedranti and Asherman, although one of George's sons remained with the business. (Courtesy Petaluma Museum.)

The roads were dusty in turn-of-the-century Petaluma, especially during the hot summer, and bars like Myer's Eagle Saloon on B Street were popular cooling-off spots. The man in the center with his elbow out is barber Al Langer. (Courtesy Petaluma Museum.)

Jack's Saloon on Main Street went in for the heavily-decorated look. (Courtesy Sonoma County Museum.)

J. Gwinn, Charles McNally, F. Steinback, and U.H. Tomasini pose in the office at the Petaluma National Savings Bank. Isaac G. Wickersham started Petaluma's first bank in 1865, on Main St., and three years later built the first bank building in Sonoma County. In 1874 it became the First National Gold Bank of Petaluma; the "Gold" was later dropped from the name. (Ed Fratini collection, courtesy Petaluma Museum.)

Inside the Petaluma National Bank, 1903, a customer waits at the side window while J. Gwinn and U.H. Tomasini stand at the center teller's booth. Notice the spittoon in the foreground. (Ed Fratini collection, courtesy Petaluma Museum.)

Some traveling peddlers came door to door. In 1882 Nellie Denman bought asparagus from the basket of a Chinese vegetable seller. Like many California communities, Petaluma had a sizeable Chinese population in the 1870s and early '80s, largely made up of railroad workers who had turned to other occupations. In the 1880s a wave of anti-Chinese hysteria swept much of California, largely fueled by competition for jobs. The hostility led to a statewide boycott of Chinese businesses early in 1886, with whites firing Chinese employees and pledging to avoid Chinese shops. In March 1886, Petalumans took the extra step of cutting off water to the Chinese section of town. Some Chinese fled to San Francisco; others quietly found work on local ranches. (Courtesy Petaluma Museum.)

Lucien "Red" Libarle, 11, and his father deliver laundry for the Lace House French Laundry, c. 1915. The Libarles moved from San Francisco to 128 Liberty Street, Petaluma, in 1915, starting the first laundry plant in the North Bay. Red's job was keeping the wheels greased and taking care of Jenny, the horse. Today Red's son Dan runs Lace House Linen Supply. (Courtesy Petaluma Museum.)

The American Barber Shop helped men keep up a dapper appearance. Among the men pictured here are Bob Adams (owner of the American Hotel), Jack Gilmore, Candy Jones, Tommy Gilmore, and Bill Russ. (Courtesy Petaluma Museum.)

A large staff was on hand to help customers inside Raymond Brothers' at 117 Main Street. The Goods included ready-to-wear (as opposed to tailored) clothes. The store offered stools for customers to rest on while looking over the merchandise in the yardage department. (Courtesy Petaluma Museum.)

Young men who worked as clerks at Raymond Brothers store, c. 1904, included the Mattei brothers, Richard (back row, center) and Valenti (front row, right). In 1907 the Mattei brothers started their own store on Kentucky Street, selling clothing for men and boys. Three-piece suits and high collars were considered standard attire for waiting on customers. (Courtesy Petaluma Museum.)

Petaluma served as the connection between shipping and rail lines for the North Bay, and its hotels like the Yosemite, the Tivoli, and the American on Main (above, center) offered both tourists and traveling merchants a place to stay. To the left of the hotel is Raymond Brothers' furniture and clothing store. (Courtesy Petaluma Museum.)

I.B. Raymond, shown here c. 1910, was the owner of Raymond Brothers', one of Petaluma's biggest clothing stores. (Courtesy Petaluma Museum.)

Mr. and Mrs. C.K. Martin (behind the counter) wait on a customer in their store, 1919. The Martins sold the store in 1920 to Baptista Pedroni, who ran it as the Petaluma Market and then changed the name to Pedroni's. (Courtesy Petaluma Museum.)

Volpi's Italian market at 122 Washington Street has been in the same place since Louis Solari moved the store there in 1908. Silvio Volpi bought it in 1925. During Prohibition, dairymen coming to sell their milk would slip into Volpi's back room for a clandestine drink. Silvio and his wife Mary (Oberto) served a basic Italian lunch to ranchers and businessmen. Their son John took over the business, and today Volpi's is a restaurant and deli. Here Mike Palucci cuts a wheel of cheese, with Josephine Nosecchi looking on. (Courtesy Petaluma Museum.)

Inside Purity Grocery, c. 1920s, canned goods that didn't fit onto shelves along the wall were piled up in pyramids on the floor, unlike today's supermarkets with parallel rows of shelves.

After World War I, local investors pledged money to build a hotel by popular subscription. Boosters for the Hotel Petaluma, c. 1925, included realtor A.W. Baker (second from left), Dr. Rogers (third from left), and three ladies on the right: Sophie Hammel, Mrs. Salb, and Hulda Schultz. (Ed Fratini collection, courtesy Petaluma Museum.)

Once the money was raised, construction of the Hotel Petaluma at the southwest corner of Washington and Kentucky went forward. The building, seen here from the Kentucky Street side c. 1930, remains there today. (Courtesy Petaluma Museum.)

Seen here is the Continental Hotel, on the south side of Western Avenue between Keller and Kentucky, c. 1940. It burned down in the mid-1960s. Next to the hotel were a bowling alley, launderette, barber, and the Shadowbox Cafe. Fire was the bane of early hotels. An 1866 fire destroyed the Franklin and Sullivan Hotels. The American Hotel, started as a boarding house in 1852, burned down in 1868 and again in 1873. (Courtesy Petaluma Museum.)

Storefronts in this 1911 building on Main Street included Guy's furniture, Jim Peeble's real estate office, Harmony music store, The Bend, and the entrance to the Moose Club, which also had rooms for the Veterans of Foreign Wars. (Courtesy Petaluma Museum.)

Car production came to a halt during World War II, when metal and tires were reserved for armaments. In 1946, Floyd Motors, the Dodge-Plymouth dealer at 301 Main Street, received its first batch of new vehicles, and customers lined up to buy them. Pictured from left to right are: painting contractor William Morris receiving his keys from owner John Floyd; salesman Joe Trigera handing keys to unknown man; and parts manager Dean Dunn standing with Petaluma school teacher Norene Campbell. (Courtesy Petaluma Museum.)

E. Ornellas owned the Acme Sheet Metal Co., where the goods on display look like giants' toys. The store on East Washington burned down in 1978. (Courtesy Petaluma Museum.)

In 1921 George and Margaret Ott bought Central Music and Stationery Store at 139 Main. They discontinued the music aspect of the store and it became simply Ott's Stationery. Here Wesley Ott (left) and Vernon Black pose with new Royal typewriters in the window of the Petaluma Boulevard store, c. 1960. (Courtesy Petaluma Museum.)

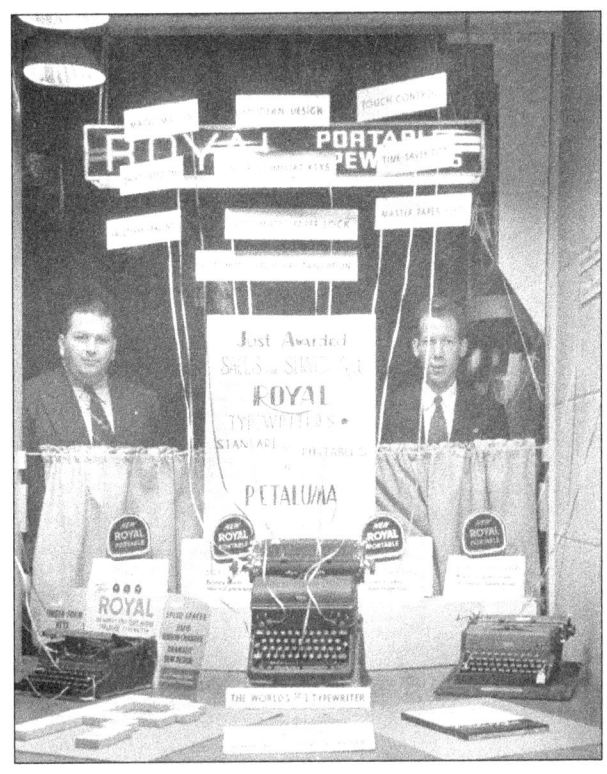

In 1911, when Charles Kelley and family stopped for gas, pumps often stood outside stores. Kelley was the owner of the Kelley Oil Warehouse. Note the spare attached to the side. Few roads were paved, and spare tires were a must. (Courtesy Petaluma Museum.)

Fred Kelley's Shell service station, pictured here in the late '40s, is a reminder of the days when a horde of attendants swooped down on your car to clean the windshield, fill your tires, and pump gas before bringing you your change. (Courtesy Petaluma Museum.)

Eight
MILITARY TRADITION

Petaluma's Company C poses in front of the Petaluma City Hall in 1904. The town's first militia, or Guard, was organized by Captain Armstrong in the late 1850s. Like many militias of this sort, the Guard was eventually absorbed into the local National Guard. (Courtesy Petaluma Museum.)

Petaluma's Company C marched in the Fourth of July parade of 1900. Doubtless some Civil War veterans marched as well. Petaluma was unique among Sonoma County towns for being staunchly pro-Union. Neighboring Santa Rosa was solidly pro-Confederate, many of its residents having migrated from Tennessee and other southern states. Few locals traveled the long distance to the fighting, and the battles were mostly fought in the editorial pages of rival newspapers. Samuel Cassiday, editor of the pro-Lincoln *Argus*, flung insults at the secessionists in Santa Rosa, while Thomas Thompson, editor of Santa Rosa's *Sonoma Democrat*, responded in kind against Petaluma and its abolitionists. Petaluma also maintained its own Union Militia, the Hueston Guard, also known as the Emmett Rifles. Union veterans living in Petaluma formed Antietam Post No. 63; the last surviving member was Petaluman Charles Wesley McDade, a native of Pennsylvania, who died in 1940.

As throngs of townspeople see them off, Petaluma's Company K assembles at the railroad yards on April 5, 1917, preparing to depart for World War I. The depot is on the far right. (Courtesy Petaluma Museum.)

Petaluman Floyd Doss (on the left) poses with his buddy, Shorty Hall, who hailed from North Dakota. They served together in France during World War I. (Courtesy Petaluma Museum.)

Larry Ruff named his B-25 "Terrible Terry," after his brother Terrance who was shot down over Rabaul in November 1943. Larry Ruff flew 72 combat missions in the South Pacific; he was killed in March 1945 when a jeep he was riding in collided with an Army truck on Biak Island. (Courtesy Petaluma Museum.)

First Lt. Robert R. Bennett, another Petaluman, was lost over North Africa with his crew in March 1943. In all, 84 men from Petaluma were killed in World War II. (Courtesy Petaluma Museum.)

Nine
CIVIC INSTITUTIONS AND THE BIG SCOOP

A town depends on local media for news about town life, including all the other institutions like police, schools, and city hall. Radio station KAFP, affectionately known as Kalling Always for Petaluma (and occasionally as Krowing Always for Petaluma), kept listeners up to date. Bill Soberanes (right) interviewed a range of personalities for the station and still writes about people for the *Argus*. (Courtesy Petaluma Museum.)

In 1853, three Weston brothers boarded a clipper in Boston, intent on founding a newspaper somewhere out west. Henry Weston (left) settled in Petaluma and in 1855 went to work for Thomas L. Thompson, publisher of the *Petaluma Journal and Sonoma County Advertiser*. Thompson, although only 17, lobbied hard for civic improvements, such as firefighting equipment, before selling the paper to Weston. In the 1860s Weston sold and then repurchased the paper, which by then was known as the *Petaluma Weekly Argus*. In 1876, William Shattuck started the *Courier*. The Olmsteds bought the *Argus* in 1900 and in 1928 merged it with the *Morning Courier* to create today's *Argus-Courier*.

Staff in the composing room of the *Argus-Courier* are, from left to right, Walter Holman, Clarence Woldemar, and Vincent Marsicano. (Courtesy Petaluma Museum.)

During the 1940s, the *Argus-Courier's* office was located on Main Street next to See's Candies. Today the paper's offices are on Petaluma Boulevard North. (Courtesy Petaluma Museum.)

Russell "Bud" Feliz taps the type frame and the metal letters cascade into a pile onto the floor. Walter Holman is standing nearby, with George Robertson in the back. Like other papers, the *Argus-Courier* later made the transition from metal type to phototypesetting, then to computer-generated copy, leaving Gutenberg's movable type behind. (Courtesy Petaluma Museum.)

Petaluma City Hall on Kentucky Street was built in 1887 at a cost of $16,000. In front is the fire department's pumper. Lincoln Primary at Fifth and B is at left rear. (Courtesy Petaluma Museum.)

City workers wrestle with debris from the city hall, which was demolished in 1955. The new city hall is on English Street. (Courtesy Petaluma Museum.)

The post office, on the northwest corner of Fourth and D Streets, is on the former site of the McNear mansion. It is now on the National Register of Historic Places and is still Petaluma's central post office. (Courtesy Petaluma Museum.)

Steel magnate Andrew Carnegie, who financed many town libraries at the turn of the century, granted Petaluma $12,500 of the $20,000 the city had requested for a new library. Another $4,000 came from public subscriptions. Construction began in 1904; masons (right) obtained sandstone for the edifice at a quarry near Roblar. (Ed Mannion collection, courtesy Petaluma Museum.)

School children line up to visit the Carnegie Library at Fourth and B Streets during annual Book Week, 1941. The library was designed by local architect Brainerd Jones in the Neo-Classical Revival style. The town's first library was started in 1867 by the Oddfellows, who turned it over to the city in 1878; the books were kept upstairs at City Hall. (Courtesy Petaluma Museum.)

In the 1970s, Petalumans approved a bond for a new library, with the understanding that the old one would be saved. It reopened its doors in 1978 as the Petaluma Historical Museum, run by the Petaluma Historical Society, which was formed in 1953. The building still lives up to the words above its entrance, "Free Public Library," as the Petaluma Historical Society maintains a research archive that is free to the public. The new library opened on East Washington in 1976. (Courtesy Petaluma Museum.)

Petaluma's first fire brigade formed in 1857; town fathers went to San Francisco to purchase a Knickerbocker Engine (now at the Petaluma Museum). By 1880 the town had six fire companies, which competed to get to the fires. James Mott (above), the Petaluma fire department's first paid employee, was killed in 1912 when an automobile exploded during a fire. Motorized fire trucks made Black Bart (above), the department's last working horse, obsolete; in 1915 he went to live on a ranch in Penngrove. (Courtesy Petaluma Museum.)

In 1912, the volunteer companies disbanded and the city assumed the task of fighting fires. Driver Toni Peters (above) parked the PFD's new motorized rig by the steps of City Hall, 1912. (Courtesy Petaluma Museum.)

Petaluma hired its first marshall, James Siddens, in 1858 and also built a three-cell "calaboose" to house the lawbreakers. By 1870 the city had 10 policemen; in 1907 the *Argus* congratulated Petaluma on being "neither a goody-goody city nor a wide open town." Two popular police chiefs of the 20th century were Mike Flohr, who left to take over as county sheriff, and his successor Robert Peters, sheriff from 1931 to 1950. When Melvin "Noonie" Del Maestro took over in 1950, the force had three cars and two motorcycles. (Courtesy Petaluma Museum.)

Postmaster Dick Dunbar demonstrates his delivery technique when faced with ferocious animals in this tongue-in-cheek ad for Halt dog repellent. Dunbar also served as the president of the Petaluma Museum. (Courtesy Petaluma Museum.)

Along with local government come those who protest its actions. Rancher Max Kortum, toting a wagonload of his grandchildren, organized the 1948 Freeway Revolt to protest the construction of a freeway through town. (Courtesy Petaluma Museum.)

Helen Putnam, who served Petaluma as school board president, mayor, and finally district supervisor, was known around town as Madame Mayor or simply "the lady with the bracelets," because she loved to wear bangles all the way up her arms. A teacher for 20 years before launching her political career, Putnam was mayor from 1965 to 1979, then ran for second district supervisor, serving two terms on the board. She died in 1984; the following year the Helen Putnam Regional Park was dedicated to her.

A rare snowfall frosted Petaluma's tropic palms, possibly during the freak storm on New Year's Day, 1916.

Hill Plaza Park between Kentucky and Petaluma Boulevard North, a block north of Washington, looks peaceful in this 1959 photo, but the land nearly became something else. Garrett Keller left it as a potential city plaza when he surveyed the area for lots in 1852. Succeeding generations proposed using the spot for a jail, a city hall, a high school, and finally, in 1960, a parking lot. Town preservationists, including historian Ed Mannion, gathered signatures to keep the spot as a city park. (Courtesy Petaluma Museum.)

Edward S. Lippitt began Petaluma's first high school in 1867 as a private enterprise. It was located on D Street between Sixth and Seventh Streets, later the site of the D Street Grammar School. The high school later became public, then moved to a second school site (above) on Keller.

The first McKinley School, at Washington and Vallejo, was built in 1911. Future Petaluma historian Ed Fratini is second from the right, in bib overalls. A new McKinley School opened in 1950 on Ellis Street. (Courtesy Petaluma Museum.)

Third graders from the Lincoln Elementary School exercise in back of the brick schoolhouse, 1897. The small boy in front in white pants is Malcolm Byce, son of the incubator manufacturer. Built in 1859 at the corner of Fifth and B Streets, it was the first schoolhouse in Sonoma County to be constructed of brick. (Courtesy Petaluma Museum.)

Sometimes called the Red Brick School, Lincoln Elementary was the town's original grammar school and was designed to serve 250 students. A new Lincoln Elementary was built on the same corner in 1911. It was designed in the Greek Revival style by famed local architect Brainerd Jones. The bricks from the old school were then reused at other building sites, including the Lasher Hatchery on North Main. (Courtesy Petaluma Museum.)

Pictured here are students gathered outside the second Petaluma High School, possibly to admire its spectacular tubular fire escape, 1894. At the turn of the century, a popular student escapade was sneaking into the fire escape and sliding down to the bottom. The building was demolished around 1920, putting an end to that particular entertainment. (Courtesy Petaluma Museum.)

When the high school population outgrew the second high school, a new PHS was built on Fair Street in 1915, at a cost of $110,000. *The Enterprise* began in 1880 as a four-page monthly newsletter and later evolved into a school yearbook. (Courtesy Petaluma Museum.)

The Petaluma High School girls' basketball team for 1916 included, from left to right: (back row) Edith Raymond, Pearl Falon, Pansy Parmiter, Iva Tazer, Georgia Murphy, and Emma Wyman; (front row) Daisy George, Ruby Merritt, Aline Barber, and Eva Falon. Basketball was one of the most popular sports for Petaluma girls at the turn of the century; PHS had a girls' team even before it formed one for the boys. (Courtesy Petaluma Museum.)

Petaluma High School's football team for 1905 included Roy Evans (front row, center), the team captain. The school's football club was formed in 1881 and at the turn of the century they were playing out-of-county teams. In 1904, for instance, PHS lost to San Rafael, reportedly because the Marin boys' shoes had cleats and the Petalumans' shoes did not. (Courtesy Petaluma Museum.)

Petaluma High cheerleaders and pep squad work the crowd during a game. In front are cheerleaders Bonnie Hawkins and Coleen Egbert. Pep squad members in back are Myrna Olson, Jayne de Brugaher, and Carolyn Spongenberg. (Courtesy Petaluma Museum.)

Several prominent ranchers put on their best suits to go and vote at rural Waugh School northeast of town, including Frank Whitlatch, L.A. Hardin, John Caltorff, and Postmaster Jim Long (women didn't join the ranks of California voters until 1920). The first Waugh School was built in 1864; the 1925 building that replaced it served as a school until 1960 and still stands at the corner of Adobe and Corona Roads. Other schools on the outskirts of Petaluma included Liberty, Lakeville, Payran, and Cinnabar, which is now a community theatre. All were established in the mid 1860s.

Private schools also played an important role in local education. St. Vincent's School on Howard Street, established in 1865, was one of the larger private schools for the children of Petaluma. (Courtesy Petaluma Museum.)

Ten
THE SOCIAL ROUND

Social life throughout Petaluma's history has included sports, bands, parades, theatricals, fairs, and activities as simple as going out for a drive. Fraternal organizations like Petaluma's IOOF (International Order of Odd Fellows) organized their own bands. This one included, from left to right: (first row) Clarence Winfield, unidentified, Lester Hollis, unidentified, and Frank Myers; (second row) Brady, unidentified, Harry Smith, unidentified, (?) Segrist, and Frank Emenegger; (third row, second from right) Horbert Park. Formed in 1854, the Petaluma IOOF was one of the town's first social organizations. (Courtesy Petaluma Museum.)

The Elite Bowling Parlor on Kentucky Street, 1903, offered indoor bowling. The most popular sports for men before the turn of the century were baseball and horse racing. Bicycling was also popular. Petaluma got a new bicycle track in 1895, although the local club, the Petaluma Wheelman, disbanded in 1897. (Courtesy Petaluma Museum.)

Raising homing pigeons was one of many hobbies that townspeople pursued. Here a Mr. Newburg, L.C. Byce (hidden behind Newburg), Malcolm Byce, and young Elwood Byce examine champion registered homing pigeons at the Byce home at 226 Liberty Street. (Courtesy Petaluma Museum.)

Dressing up to go calling on friends and relations was one of the pleasures of early 20th century Petaluma. The young people in their best clothes at the Bodwell ranch near Lakeville are, from left to right, Austin Sperry, Beda Sperry, Horace Sperry, and Elizabeth Bodwell. (Courtesy Petaluma Museum.)

When the car replaced the horse and wagon, just going out for a spin around the orchard was a new thrill. (Courtesy Petaluma Museum.)

The Kenilworth Park Club boasted a clubhouse and bar where you could sit at leisure and watch the races. Club owner Harry Stover named the place after one of his prize horses. After Stover's death in 1910 his estate became the Sonoma-Marin Fairgrounds. (Courtesy Petaluma Museum.)

Mrs. Hyde practiced her swing on the golf course, c. 1920. Note the sturdy saddle shoes, which were still in fashion in the 1950s. (Courtesy Petaluma Museum.)

Baseball teams sponsored by businesses like the Golden Eagle Mill were popular. The Alerts, the 1903 team of the town's best players, included: catcher (?) Waymire, Bill Evart, Ernst Guyon, Toots Baldwin, Clyde Healy, William Keneally, manager Willett Hopkins (in bowler), Robert Ayers, Emmett Howard, Tom Caulfield, and Jack Lauritzen. (Courtesy Petaluma Museum.)

A Leghorn batter slides safely into home during a 1947 game against the DeLuca Real Estate team. There was also a Leghorn Football team. (Courtesy Petaluma Museum.)

Petaluma's semi-pro football team, the Leghorns, played from 1946 to 1958, and during those years they were the main topic of sports conversation in town. Young men returning from World War II started the Leghorn club football team. Nearly all the players were former Petaluma High or St. Vincent students, and as a result town loyalty to the team was intense, especially since they won so often. By 1949, they were good enough to join the semi-pro Western Football Association. Coached by Gene Benedetti until 1950, the Leggies faced colorfully named opponents like the San Francisco Windbreaks, the Treasure Island Pirates, and the rival Santa Rosa Bonecrushers. (Courtesy Sonoma County Museum.)

The team's 12-year record was 88 wins, 32 losses, and 4 ties. San Francisco papers sent sports writers to cover the games, and Leghorns scores made the national wire services. (Courtesy Sonoma County Museum.)

Tackle Butch Burtner came up with the idea of an Egg Bowl as a season finale, with proceeds going to charity. The team disbanded in 1958, as interest in local games waned with the advent of television. (Courtesy Sonoma County Museum.)

They're off and running for the Petaluma Marathon, as contestants race past the Petaluma Adobe. Ed Fratini and the Spartans sports club established the first official marathon west of the Mississippi, holding the initial event in summer of 1935. The race drew internationally known runners, including Jesse Van Zant of the San Francisco Olympic Club and Chinese runner Wang Ching Ling. At left, Fratini, an avid runner himself, congratulates Van Zant, winner of the 1947 marathon. Fratini, who worked at the Petaluma Wells-Fargo bank, was a life-long athlete, running his last race at age 78. He was also one of Petaluma's premier amateur historians. He died in 1993, at the age of 91. (Courtesy Petaluma Museum.)

Fraternal organizations were an important aspect of social life. Here members of the Lions Club pose beside their "MGM Lion" float in a parade in front of the California Theatre at Washington and Keller. Participants included Mayor William Farrell, Sandy McFadden, jeweler John Camm, Dr. Stuart Peoples, undertaker John Mount, and grocer Henry Gray. Formed in 1925, the Petaluma Lions built a bandstand in Walnut Park and sponsored chapters of the Campfire Girls and the Boy Scouts. (Courtesy Petaluma Museum.)

The granite fountain commissioned by the Women's Christian Temperance Union still sits at the corner of Western and Main, having survived a hit from an errant Volkswagen (the bug was totaled). An inscription on the side reads, "Total abstinence is the way to handle the alcohol problem." Petaluma's WCTU was formed in 1879; Petaluman Edward Lippitt also sponsored the Lippitt Temperance Club, offering sober activities for young people to steer them away from alcohol-related parties. (Courtesy Petaluma Museum.)

With a river right on their doorstep, Sea Scouts grew up practicing their nautical skills on the Petaluma River as well as San Francisco Bay. Scouts also went camping over the hill at Olema Scout Camp near Pt. Reyes. (Courtesy Petaluma Museum.)

The Hill Opera House provided a venue for both amateur and professional theatricals. (Courtesy Petaluma Museum.)

Petalumans with ties to ethnic communities formed support organizations. John and Maria Davina (later Dabner), originally from the Azores, founded the Holy Ghost Society in 1891 for the town's Portuguese community. Their band posed outside the Holy Ghost Hall, c. 1895. The society celebrated its centennial in 1991. (Petaluma Holy Ghost collection, courtesy Sonoma County Museum.)

Mary Maio (Parreira) was selected as the Holy Ghost Society's queen for 1916. Other ethnic communities had their own clubs, such as the Hermann Sons for German immigrants, formed in Petaluma in 1901, and the Danish Society. (Petaluma Holy Ghost collection, courtesy Sonoma County Museum.)

James M. Hall's family got him all dressed in a suit and a white bow tie for his formal portrait at age four and a half. (Courtesy Petaluma Museum.)

One aspect of social life is having your photo taken. In the days before high-speed film, this meant getting dressed up and standing or sitting very still during a long camera exposure. Leland Myers, age five, posed with his eight-year-old sister Marie (later Mrs. John Watkins) in 1905. Myers later became the druggist at L&M Pharmacy as well as mayor of Petaluma. (Ed Mannion collection, courtesy Petaluma Museum.)

Bill Deiss and his Haywire Orchestra, here tuning up their instruments in front of Triple A, played for local events like the Sonoma-Marin Fair. Left to right are Guido Boccaleoni on accordion, Toby Tobias, unidentified, Bill Deiss at the microphone, (?) Robinson on fiddle, Ed Gundstrom, and Ben Righetti with his banjo. (Courtesy Petaluma Museum.)

Community breakfasts in Center Park were an annual event for the Sonoma-Marin Fair. Bill Deiss and his Haywire Orchestra are playing on a platform in the background, near the State theatre. (Courtesy Petaluma Museum.)

Three gals (including Pat Ceresa, center, dressed as a chicken) climbed aboard a tractor on their way to the Sonoma-Marin Fair. The fair of the state's Fourth Agricultural District began in 1868 west of town. By 1880 the town purchased a hundred acres for a fairground on the eastern edge of town. Harry Stover bought the site in 1887 and ran it as a private track. In 1936, district fairs were revived and the city repurchased the property, adding new judging rings, barns, and a restaurant in the 1950s. (Courtesy Petaluma Museum.)

The first Petaluma churches to form were the Methodist Church in 1849 and the Baptist in 1853. Other denominations soon followed as the town grew. St. Vincent's Catholic parish was formed in 1857 and its first church was built the same year. The second St. Vincent's church (above) was constructed in 1885 and in 1925 was moved to Western Avenue to become the Elim Lutheran Church.

The third and current St. Vincent's Church (right) was built with double steel reinforcement, because the priest, Father James Kiely, had witnessed the destruction of his Novato church in the 1906 quake. The first mass was celebrated on Christmas Eve, 1926.

The Methodist Episcopal Church was on Western Avenue between Keller and Liberty Streets. This building now serves the United Methodist congregation. (Courtesy Petaluma Museum.)

Petaluma's Jewish families gathered at the Jewish Community Center on Western Avenue for dinners and other events. The first Jewish families came in the 1860s and in 1864 founded the first congregation, B'nai Israel. In 1915 several Jewish families arrived in Petaluma to establish a community on socialist principles. Their aim was to create a healthy rural life as an alternative for refugees fleeing the sweatshops in the eastern U.S. By 1925 there were a hundred Jewish families and a community center. (Courtesy Petaluma Museum.)

www.ingramcontent.com/pod-product-compliance
Lightning Source LLC
Chambersburg PA
CBHW080905100426
42812CB00007B/2162